D1824419

a question of Love

Homosexuality
A Biblical Perspective

a question of Love

Homosexuality
A Biblical Perspective

Answers to questions on Homosexuality by
Dr Angelo Grazioli, MB, ChB, BTh (Hons)

CWR, Waverley Abbey House, Waverley Lane, Farnham, Surrey GU9 8EP

National Distributors

UK (and countries not listed below)
STL, PO Box 300, Kingstown Broadway, Carlisle, Cumbria CA3 0QS, UK Tel: 0345 413500 (local rate call) Outside UK (44) 1228 611745

AUSTRALIA: CMC Australasia, PO Box 519, Belmont, Victoria 3216 Tel: (03) 5241 3288

CANADA: CMC Distribution Ltd., PO Box 7000, Niagara on the Lake, Ontario L0S 1J0 Tel: 1 800 325 1297

INDIA: Full Gospel Literature Stores, 254 Kilpauk Garden Road, Chennai 600010 Tel: (44) 644 3073

KENYA: Keswick Bookshop, PO Box 10242, Nairobi Tel: (02) 331692/226047

MALAYSIA: Salvation Book Centre (M), 23 Jalan SS2/64, Sea Park, 47300 Petaling Jaya, Selangor Tel: (3) 7766411

NEW ZEALAND: CMC New Zealand Ltd., PO Box 949, 205 King Stree South, Hastings Tel: (6) 8784408, Toll free: 0800 333639

NIGERIA: FBFM, (Every Day with Jesus), Prince's Court, 37 Ahmed Onibudo Street, PO Box 70952, Victoria Island Tel: 01 2617721/61683

REPUBLIC OF IRELAND: Scripture Union, 40 Talbot Street, Dublin 1 Tel: (01) 8363764

SINGAPORE: Campus Crusade Asia Ltd., 315 Outram Road, 06-08 Tan Boon Liat Building, Singapore 169074 Tel: (65) 222 3640

SRI LANKA: Christombu Investments, 27 Hospital Street, Colombo 1 Tel: (1) 433142/328909

SOUTH AFRICA: Struik Christian Books (Pty Ltd), PO Box 193, Maitland 7405, Cape Town Tel: (021) 551 5900

USA: CMC Distribution, PO Box 644, Lewiston, New York 14092-064< Tel: 1 800 325 1297

A Question of Love
A lightly edited transcript of a seminar by Angelo Grazioli

Copyright © CWR 1998

Design and Typesetting: CWR Production
Printed in Great Britain by Clifford Frost

ISBN 1 85345 126 6

Unless otherwise identified, all Scripture quotations in this publication are from the Holy Bible: New International Version (NIV). Copyright © 1973, 1978, 1984, International Bible Society.

CONTENTS

INTRODUCTION

Homosexuality is one of the most complex subjects I think I have ever come across and there are many different views in the Church on the issue. Because of lack of understanding as to the Biblical position on homosexuality many Christians find it difficult to hold meaningful conversations on the subject and this has led, all too often, to prejudice towards those living a homosexual lifestyle. Our aim in this book is to lay down some clear Biblical principles on the subject in a question and answer format which will give a clear understanding of God's view on the subject and lead to a greater compassion towards homosexual persons.

I am sure that this book will be a useful reference work for all Christians including those involved in counselling and pastoral care.

I know of no-one in whom I have more confidence to be able to deal with the subject of homosexuality from a Biblical perspective than Dr Angelo Grazioli. Dr Grazioli lives in South Africa and is the Director of the Sex Education and Dysfunction Unit of South Africa. He holds degrees in Medicine and Theology. He is a broadcaster in South Africa and has appeared many times on television. Dr Grazioli is also a consultant editor for *Carer and Counsellor,* CWR's counselling journal, and lectures regularly at Waverley Abbey House, CWR's Christian training centre in the south of England.

The manuscript for this book is taken from one of the lectures that Dr Grazioli gave in Waverley Abbey House to a specially invited audience. Dr Grazioli has absolute confidence in the Scriptures and this publication will help you to track your way through this complex subject and lead you to a Biblical understanding of how to deal with homosexuality. I believe you will find this publication useful, helpful and encouraging.

Selwyn Hughes

PREFACE

Homosexuals, or people in sympathy with homosexuality as a valid sexual activity, often ask tough and important questions that deserve sensitive, well-thought-out answers. 1 Peter 3:15 tells us to "always be prepared to give an answer to everyone who asks you to give the reason for the hope that you have. But do this with gentleness and respect." Gentleness and respect should always characterise what we say and do, and I hope that the answers I give to the questions posed in this booklet will exhibit those same qualities.

So what are the kind of questions that people ask about this subject? What, especially, do homosexuals say about it? Some examples would be, "If God loves me so much, why does he say that I cannot be gay? All I am trying to do is meet my deep, heartfelt need for love, just like everyone else. So why can't I do it with a man instead of a woman?" Or, "Being gay is completely natural for me, why does God expect me to act in an unnatural way? It would be unnatural for me to act as a heterosexual. The Bible was written by a bunch of straight and bigoted Jews who were trying to preserve a bloodline. It has very little relevance to me today." Or, "You say I should not be gay because the Bible says so, but the Bible also says that you should not eat oysters, or pork, or rare steak, but you do all those things. So why are you picking on me for being gay, when you do not abide by everything the Bible says yourself? Aren't you being a hypocrite?"

Difficult and important issues!

Angelo Grazioli

What does the Bible say about homosexuality?

In the Bible there are three categories of passage that refer to homosexuality. The first is historical references, the second legal references, and finally New Testament references.

Historical references

There are two, fairly well known historical passages about homosexuality in the Old Testament. The first is in Genesis 19:1–11. Here we have the incident in Sodom where Lot offers hospitality to two messengers from God. The men of the city demand the surrender of the guests in order to have sex with them. Lot tries to talk them out of it, but fails, so instead offers his two virgin daughters to them. This does not satisfy the mob and Lot himself is soon in danger, but is saved by the intervention of the heavenly visitors. The destruction of Sodom follows immediately.

How do gay theologians explain this passage?

1. It deals only with myth and culture.
2. It is not about homosexuality, but hospitality issues.
3. It is not about homosexuality, but hostility or violent sexuality.

Let's look at these explanations in turn.

First, the belief that this is myth and culture. Some people do maintain that the story of Sodom is the product of cultural prejudice of the time, born out of a desire to discourage the Jews from homosexuality. Theirs was a very heterosexual society, and, as the chosen race, they saw coming from their loins the bloodline from whom the Messiah himself would eventually come into the world. So the whole concept of homosexuality was foreign to Jewish people. As a result, this Sodom myth arose to discourage homosexual activity.

If we regard Scripture as the work of man alone, then we might be able to accept this argument. But if we believe Scripture to be the inspired Word of God, then we cannot accept that we would find myth in the Bible. This argument has more to do with the reader's attitude toward Scripture. Is it the infallible, inspired Word of God? If not, then we would have to accept that the writers could introduce their own ideas and myths. If we believe it is inspired by the Holy Spirit, then there is no room for myth and culture in it. Yes, it is imperative that we understand what is written in the cultural and historical context peculiar to the writers, so that we do not misunderstand the message. However, to accept the figures of speech and examples used by human writers, is not to deny that they were under divine guidance and therefore writing only that which God would have them write.

Secondly, some people maintain that the words in verse 5 of this passage taken to mean "to have sex with" are, in various versions of the Bible, translated as "to know" and simply mean "to get acquainted with" rather than having any sexual connotations. These critics say that the men of Sodom realised belatedly that they had been rude to Lot's guests who had arrived in the city in the evening. It was now the middle of the night and they had still failed to show any hospitality, so they came to Lot at night to make up for their discourtesy and to get "to know" the strangers.

Why can I not agree with this explanation? If hospitality was what was really motivating this crowd of men, why did Lot offer his two virgin daughters to them? He would in effect be saying, "It's too late to show hospitality to my guests, they are tired and in bed, show hospitality to my virgin daughters instead. That will make up for it"! That just does not make sense.

And why would Lot call this belated, apparent offer of hospitality wicked? Why should he be so offended by the proposal of the mob? And why did the men get angry with Lot, accuse him of being judgmental and threaten him, if he was just trying to help them with being hospitable rather than trying to oppose their sexual intent?

The whole explanation of this incident being a question of hospitality just does not stand proper scrutiny.

Thirdly, was this incident a question of hostility, or violent sexuality, rather than just homosexuality? The argument supported by some gay theologians in this respect is that it is not homosexuality that is here being condemned, but it is the fact that it was going to be forced on guests who did not wish to engage in homosexual acts. It is the violence associated with it, the lack of consent, which is being condemned in this passage, they maintain.

Is God concerned with the act or the motivation behind it?

This crucial third argument assumes that homosexual acts are okay as far as God is concerned as long as the individuals involved are consenting adults, but is this true? Leviticus 18:22 and 20:13 define male homosexuality as detestable and worthy of the death penalty. 1 Kings 14:24 and 15:12 condemn male prostitutes, and their removal is seen as a sign of spiritual reformation in the land.

Gay theologians, however, argue that these passages refer to homosexuality in a religious context, as part of religious worship, and that is what made it detestable. It is the same as any other form of pagan worship, or even marrying foreign brides, which was also condemned. Homosexuality without religious overtones, they say, is not condemned, just as homosexuality without violence and force is not condemned.

The book of Leviticus, however, condemns other things such as incest, adultery, prostitution and bestiality. As difficult as it might be to conceive, incest and adultery could be seen as very warm and tender, and both can be heterosexual. Sometimes these acts are carried out in a very warm and caring environment, but they are still condemned in Leviticus. No, incest, adultery, prostitution, bestiality, homosexuality are condemned as acts, no matter what the motivation behind them. This emphasis on the act itself being condemned, rather than the motivation behind it, occurs again and again in Scripture, as we will see.

Now let's take a look at the second historical passage – Judges 19:22–26. Here a traveller arrives late in Gibea with his concubine and servant. They are offered hospitality by an elderly resident, but the wicked men of the city demand that the traveller be brought out so that they can have sex with him. The host refuses and offers them instead his virgin daughter and his guest's concubine. The concubine is raped and subsequently killed. Judgment follows in this case in the form of military action.

There are obvious similarities between this passage and the one in Genesis 19. The major difference is that the Sodom incident occurred before Moses was given the law on Mount Sinai. So although you could argue that in Genesis there was no written law and Lot was acting out of some kind of moral indignation, you cannot say that of the passage in Judges. The people in Judges definitely had the law and were responding according to it. They were not simply responding from cultural or personal bias.

It is also very important to note that neither historical reference mentions homosexual orientation, desires or psychology. It is only the physical act which is condemned. Wickedness here defines the act, not the orientation, thoughts or desires. The passages do not say that God was against those homosexual men, that he did not love them as human beings, or that he was unaware of their feelings. What he hates and condemns is behaviour which robs us of fellowship with him, that sin which deprives us of the abundant life he desires for us.

Legal references

Before we begin to look at these references, we need to ask why God gives us laws at all. Deuteronomy 10 says he gives us laws for our own good. The problem is that we so often try to decide what is good for us, rather than heed what God decrees. In dealing with homosexuality, we must resist the temptation to put words into God's mouth, to redefine Scripture according to our own preference and perspective, our own idea of what is loving and justified. That, of course, applies whether we consider ourselves to be heterosexual or homosexual.

For example, God says adultery is sin, so we dare not comfort a grieving widow by having sex with her, no matter how loved and validated that may make her feel, or how natural an expression of love that may seem to us. There is no justified or sinless way to commit adultery. Similarly, there is no justified or sinless way to engage in homosexual acts.

There is much confusion about the legal passages concerning homosexuality, and the reason is that many fail to recognise that there are five different types of laws given by God.

1. Physical laws.

These are the cause and effect laws which God has built into the universe, such as gravity, the laws of chemistry, and so on.

2. Moral laws.

These are about absolute right and wrong and are rooted in the very nature of God. They are enshrined in the Ten Commandments.

3. Civil laws.

These are moral laws which are translated into the government of a group of people. Civil laws are moral laws made into legal, binding pacts between individuals. The severity of the penalty prescribed by these civil laws always illustrates the importance of the underlying moral law.

4. Ceremonial laws.

These relate to the religious life of people and regulate that religious life. Ceremonial laws are symbols of spiritual realities which are not yet fulfilled. When those spiritual realities are fulfilled, the ceremonial laws cease. For example, animal sacrifices were meant to symbolise the covering up of sin by shedding blood. But when Jesus came and shed his blood once for all for sin, blood sacrifices were no longer necessary.

5. Circumstantial laws.

These laws apply only to special circumstances, and only for as long as those circumstances exist. An example of this would be the regulations for collecting Manna that Israel was given before entering the Promised Land. Once they entered Canaan, the Manna stopped and the laws to do with its handling therefore also ceased.

So civil, ceremonial and circumstantial laws may change and become obsolete, but physical and particularly moral laws are immutable. Christ came to fulfil and live out God's moral laws, not do away with them.

How do the laws in the Old Testament apply to homosexuality?

The first legal reference to homosexuality is in Leviticus 18:22: "Do not lie with a man as one lies with a woman; that is detestable." The second is in Leviticus 20:13: "If a man lies with a man as one lies with a woman, both of them have done what is detestable. They must be put to death; their blood will be on their own heads."

There are important things to notice about these references. First, these are civil laws which embody a moral law. Civil laws can cease, can change from country to country, and can be righteous or unrighteous depending on how well they embody and express the underlying moral laws. But the underlying moral law, which in this case condemns homosexual activity, never changes. Secondly the penalty for homosexuality was death, underscoring the severity of the transgression. If you were caught eating shellfish, you were unclean until evening. If you were caught in a homosexual act, you were dead by evening. Homosexual acts are seen as a very serious breach of moral law. They strike at the heart of the nature of God as entrenched in his law.

Note again that there is no reference in these passages to emotions, tendencies, temptations or desires. These laws deal with homosexual acts, no matter what the mindset or inclination of the individual at the time.

New Testament references

In Romans 1 we have a description of human beings' foolish rebellion against God and the consequent desire to sin because of that rebellion. As a result, God gave them over to shameful lusts. Women had sex with women, and men committed indecent acts with other men.

What do we learn from this passage? First we note again that it is male with male, and female with female sexual acts which are condemned, not same sex love or feelings. Secondly, feelings follow actions. Men abandoned natural heterosexual function and then were inflamed with lust for other men. They committed indecent acts, so God gave them over to the lust that naturally followed. The desire to sin came first, then the act, then the lust for more. Thirdly, lusting is different from orientation. Lust is different from attraction, or a love for the same sex. This passage talks about the lust which results from willingly abandoning what God decrees to be natural for unnatural sexual acts. That is the real issue.

Loving the same sex is nowhere condemned in Scripture, in fact it is a command that came from the mouth of Jesus himself when he said that we were to love our neighbours, be they male or female. But having sex with the same sex is punished by God giving the people over to ongoing lust for the same sex, according to Romans 1.

The second New Testament reference is 1 Timothy 1:9–11: "The law is made not for the righteous but for lawbreakers and rebels ... for adulterers and perverts." The word used for pervert is the same word used for homosexual elsewhere in Scripture.

From this passage emerge more points to ponder. First, homosexuality is sin. It is listed with a whole lot of other sins, all as obviously sinful as homosexuality. Secondly, action versus feeling is again distinguished. There is no reference to the feelings or dispositions of any of the people who commit any of the sins listed. It is the act alone which is condemned. Thirdly, we see that homosexuality is no worse than any of the other sins listed. Homosexuality is simply listed together with the other sins, and not given here a special ranking all of its own.

The third New Testament reference is 1 Corinthians 6:9–11: "Do you not know that the wicked will not inherit the kingdom of God? Do not be deceived: Neither the sexually immoral nor idolaters nor adulterers nor male prostitutes nor homosexual offenders ... will inherit the kingdom of God ... and that is what some of you were. But you were washed, you were sanctified, you were justified in the name of the Lord Jesus Christ and by the Spirit of our God."

From this passage we see, as difficult as it may be to accept, that you cannot be saved and be a practising homosexual at the same time. None of these people, says the passage, will inherit the kingdom of God. Unrepentant, wilfully practising homosexuals can be deceived into believing that they are doing something loving, that they have an excuse, but according to this passage, they will not enter the kingdom of God. It is not their love for a fellow human being that condemns them, but the sin of sex with a person of their own gender. Like all other unrepentant wilful sinners, they can be deceived into believing that they are doing something loving, that they have an excuse, but they will not enter the kingdom of God.

The word which Paul uses here for both the male prostitutes and the homosexual offenders is *arsenokoites*, a composite word from *arseno* – the male – and *Koites* – coitus. In Greek there are different words to convey different ideas of homosexual acts and same sex attractions. For example, *paiederastes* is a lover of boys; *paidophthros* carries the idea of a corrupter of boys; *arrenomanes* holds the idea of someone who is mad after males. But Paul chooses the word *arsenokoites*, which simply means male with male sex. This is a very specific and unequivocal choice of word, which excludes orientation, feelings and consent, but simply focuses on the act.

What we also see from this passage is that homosexuals can change. They were made clean and justified before God. Isn't that glorious? There is real hope for all sinners, including those who commit homosexual acts.

What is homosexuality?

Very often people use the wrong terminology when discussing homosexuality. They get themselves, and others, confused simply because they do not really understand what homosexuality is.

What's love got to do with it?

90% of the people who come to see me for therapy for sexual dysfunction really have problems with love. They are physically healthy, but they are not functioning or enjoying their sexuality because of problems with their relationship. They suffer the consequences of a faulty love life. I believe that the best definition of love is to be found in the Bible. There are five words used in the original texts that are translated as love and which, when put into practice, form the five pillars of a good, healthy, dynamic, growing relationship.

The first word is *eros*, which is often understood as erotic love, but in its original Hebrew root had more to do with a deep desire to share, to dream with, to be romantically attached to. It is what we call romance.

Is homosexuality a romantic bond between two people of the same sex? No. Two people of the same sex can have deep romantic love for each other. For some it is a little difficult to visualise two men being romantically in love with each other. I remember going on a camping trip with a friend and his family. When our wives and kids were fast asleep, we would lie looking up at the stars, talking about our dreams and different things that were happening in our lives. It was cosy, very warm, very romantic, but there was nothing homosexual about it. Recent history includes a so called "age of romanticism", when men dressed and behaved in certain ways which may seem odd to us today, but were considered masculine then and had nothing to do with homosexual activity. The romantic sharing of music, art and poetry can be enjoyed by people of the same sex without erotic contact. Romance is not what homosexuality is all about.

The second type of love which human beings can experience is security, dependability and trustworthiness. It is the sort of security a child feels in a happy, caring family. I have these feelings of security about my Dad. I know he will come through for me if I ever need anything, either practically or emotionally. This love often flourishes between men in times of war, and between women under similar stressful conditions. But again, this love has nothing to do with homosexuality of itself.

The third type of love has to do with fellowship and cameraderie. It is the ability to share ourselves deeply with one another, to be vulnerable to each other, but also to be able to resolve differences and disagreements in a healthy way. Is this "best friend" kind of love what homosexuality is about? No. Men and women can have this kind of love for someone of the same sex. Jonathan and David are a good example of this deep same sex love bond.

Jesus had a best friend in John, and there was nothing homosexual about that.

Unconditional, non-demanding love is the fourth kind. It is the kind of love a parent might have for a child in a permanent vegetative state. The child is loved without expecting anything in return. He is loved unconditionally. Is it that kind of love which defines homosexuality?

Obviously not! A lot of people choose to exercise that kind of love for people of the same sex, but would not be considered homosexual because of it.

And finally we come to sexual love. Here I want to draw a distinction between what I call "sexual intercourse" and "coitus".

Sexual intercourse/coitus

Intercourse here stands for interaction. What I mean by sexual intercourse is the sexual interaction between a man and a woman by virtue of the fact that one is male and the other female. Sexual, in other words, by way of gender, not genitals. It is anything a male might say or do to a female that communicates that she is desirable, attractive, valuable, noted and special. Anything that makes her feel good as a woman, from a kiss to a remark, a gesture or a compliment. It is anything a female says or does to a male that identifies and defines him as a man as she interacts with his masculinity.

Coitus is something else. It is the physical act. You need minimum technical proficiency to get coitus right, not so sexual intercourse. Sexual intercourse, on the other hand, is an art because it changes throughout a relationship, growing and adapting to the couple's age and circumstances. It grows from a lifetime of good romance, security, companionship, expressions of love, good conflict solving and good communication. It is masculinity and femininity in action at their best.

Different people prefer different terminologies. Some prefer the terms "intimacy" and "sex". Some talk of "intercourse" and "outercourse". All are attempting to name the real difference between expressions of love rooted in sexuality and genital sexual acts. Please accept my preferred terminology for the sake of clarity in these brief answers.

Couples come to see me who have been married for many years, who know everything there is to know about coitus, but know nothing about sexual intercourse. They know how to express their sexuality, their masculinity and femininity at its most intimate in the physical act, but take that "breasts and genitals" aspect out and they have very little idea what to do or say to express their love for each other.

So is homosexuality sexual intercourse? No. Sexual intercourse between people of the same sex occurs all the time. Men at the pub express their masculinity in a way that is designed to interact with other men and build up their masculinity. Women have their own ways of achieving those same ends when they get together with other women. Homosexuality as Scripture defines it is coitus between people of the same sex. If you sodomise, have oral sex, or masturbate someone of the same sex, you are engaging in a homosexual act.

Homosexual, heterosexual, homophyllic, heterophyllic

If you love someone of the same sex, be it with romance, security, companionship, unconditionally, or in sexual intercourse as I have described it, then you are what in my profession I would call "homophyllic" from *homo* – same sex – and *phyllic* – lover of. Someone who loves somebody of the same sex is homophyllic; someone who has coitus with somebody of the same sex is engaging in a homosexual act.

Different people prefer different terminologies. Some prefer to talk about "practising homosexuals" versus "abstinent or celibate homosexuals". Others differentiate between "gay" and "homosexual". I find these particular words too vague and misused in common usage, and prefer the terms "homosexual" and "homophyllic".

One of the most deceptive lies of the century is that "homosexual" defines what you are. Using the term loosely in this fashion denies the very distinction which Scripture clearly draws between the act and the orientation. Whether we call it "homosexual and homophyllic" or "practising and abstaining homosexual" is not really important, but there is a very real difference between loving someone of the same sex, and having sex with that person.

One of the saddest, most tragic cases I have ever dealt with was that of a fifty-four-year-old man who told me that he was a Christian and a homosexual. "I can't stand it anymore," he said. "Will you please help me?"

"When did it begin?" I asked.

"Earlier, I was a youth leader at church and they used to call me 'The Pied Piper' because children used to gather around me. Wherever I went, I had a horde of kids with me", he replied.

"Okay," I said, "when did it become homosexual?"

"Right from the beginning the kids would come to me because they wanted to tell me things and share their hearts in a way they wouldn't even do with their parents", he replied. "I wanted to put my arms around them and say, 'I care for you. I love you. I'll help you'."

So I repeated my question, "When did it become homosexual?", but he didn't understand what I was trying to say. When I explained the difference between practising and non-practising, or in my terminology, the homophyllic and the homosexual, he got angry with me.

"Did you understand me to say that I'm a paedophile?" he asked disappointedly.

In fact, he had never done anything homosexual with a boy, or for that matter, with an adult. There was not a homosexual hair on his head. But he loved, deeply and truly loved, people of the same sex. He should have been a full time youth pastor, or at the very least, a teacher. Instead he went into computer system analysis research, so as to get as far away from people, particularly men, as he could.

His was a wasted life. A true Afrikaaner from the countryside, red-blooded, and, for somebody from that culture and environment, so unusually gifted by God with the ability to deeply love and care for other men. Sadly he bought the lie of the devil that because he could love so truly and deeply somebody of the same sex, that made him a homosexual.

There were at least two women who sensed that there was something very special about this man, and who wanted to pursue a relationship with him, but he fought them off. He said, "I would have loved to get married when I was younger, but it's not fair for me to marry and saddle a woman with a homosexual husband." The lie of the devil exacted its toll.

I remember falling in love with a man when I was about fourteen or fifteen years old – a geography teacher at my school. If someone had asked me if I loved him, I would have had to say, "I suppose so. I've never felt that strongly about someone, particularly someone of the same sex." But if questioned further about the basis for that love – was it based on romance, friendship or the need for security, I would have replied with a "no" to all of these. Was it unconditional love? I couldn't even spell the word at that time! Coitus? I would have said, "Are you crazy? I don't want to have sex with him in any form or fashion."

So on what was my love for him based? Well, he was an accomplished athlete who could turn female heads and I was an uncoordinated teenager. I was infatuated with the man, with what he represented. It was what I have described as sexual intercourse, male to male, which attracted me. I wanted to model myself after him. He was all that a man should be to my teenage eyes. I enjoyed being with him and loved the attention he gave me. When I was with him I felt alive and vibrant as a male. Mine was a homophyllic love, but not a homosexual love.

Is homosexuality genetic?

As a child I liked to write poetry and enjoyed the classics. I didn't enjoy rugby, and found cricket boring – virtually a sin in South Africa. I would much rather sit and enjoy a play than rock music. In today's terminology, I would have been regarded as a nerd. Now the girls do not have a lot of time for nerds, and so I would not have had much opportunity to exercise my sexuality, my sexual intercourse with girls, I would only have exercised it with boys who were also nerds. And so I fell in love with this geography teacher, this big, strapping athlete. And if somebody had asked me, "Haven't you always felt like this about boys, rather than girls?", I might well have answered "Yes".

The conclusion that some would have drawn from my answer was that I was born that way, that it was genetic. And that is a classic example of not understanding the terminology. How can sodomising, having oral sex, or masturbating, or any form of coitus be in your genes? Your orientation may be more or less homophyllic, that is a given fact. But what you do with your genitals is your choice.

If homosexuality is genetic, how can one explain hundreds of thousands of people through the centuries, on record, changing from heterosexuality to homosexuality, or homosexual to heterosexual behaviour, without changing their genetic material? Did they wake up one night when suddenly something fell out of the sky to change their genes?

I remember once at a world congress of sexology in Heidelberg, Germany, a speaker announcing, "I am going to prove to you with my latest research that homosexuality is genetic." And seven hundred delegates stood up and walked out.

Only about twenty or thirty gay activists stayed behind to confront him. I stayed around at the back of the hall because I thought they were going to lynch him. They were shouting, "If there is anyone genetically different here, it's you! We are perfectly healthy human beings. Don't dare tell us that there is something genetically different with us. We are men who choose to have sex with other men. We are free to make that choice. But we are as genetically male and normal as all other men."

If I had bought the lie that I was born with a predisposition towards homosexuality, it would have been a relatively easy step to accept an invitation, for example, to a gay club. And what would I, as an ignorant teenager, have found at the gay club? A bunch of very warm, very loving, very kind, intelligent, gifted, soft-hearted people who would have expressed interest and appreciation in the things that I enjoyed, like poetry and drama. I would have found romance. I would have found a group of people who had been discriminated against, been ostracised, who would have rallied around me and made me one of their own. I would have found security, fellowship, true soul mates who loved me as a man. I would have found true, unconditional love, and tremendous sexual intercourse, maybe for the first time in my life. I would no longer have felt like a nerd.

If this scenario had taken place in my life, for the first time I would have felt like a man, but it would only have been a matter of time before somebody made sexual advances, and coitus is coitus, orgasm is orgasm, and if it feels good, I must be homosexual. So I come out of the closet. Once I am out of the closet, it is very difficult to get back in. Another victory for the prince of deception! All I was hungry for all those years was love, but because I never understood the difference between love and coitus, I would have been caught in a gay lifestyle, the only alternative apparently natural and open to me. I would have bought the lie.

Why do people become homosexuals?

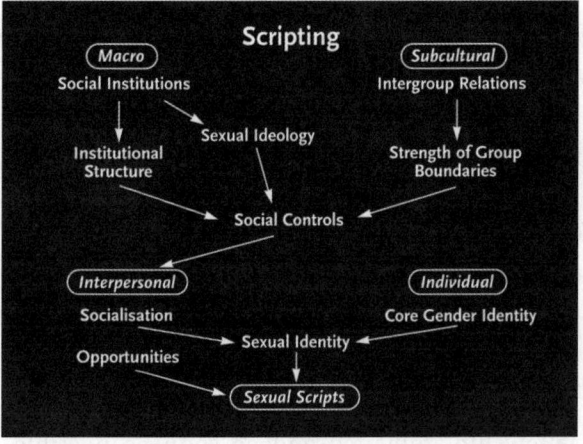

Because of what I have described, please be very careful not to assume that I am suggesting that this is the only way that someone becomes a homosexual. If you study the literature, you will find many different ways. When I lecture professionally on the subject, I probably come up with about fifteen possible ways in which people can end up in a gay lifestyle. Sometimes there is abuse. Sometimes there is a dominant parent or a very weak or absent parent, which leads to certain unconscious and, only much later, conscious decisions. Other times it may be sheer curiosity that causes people to experiment with homosexuality, only to find that they like it and stay with it. There are many different ways.

But it is possible to see how a hunger for love very often lies behind a critical choice. And it is very important to understand that this is not confined to homosexuals. Heterosexuals experience it all the time. Why do you think so many people have sex outside of marriage? Because they are looking for love, for security, fellowship, romance and as soon as possible. Coital intimacy easily creates an illusion of romance. Giving oneself to another in full coital union easily creates a quick sense of security and commitment. Coitus can be easily substituted for competent communication and conflict solving skills to create an illusion of true companionship. But it is all just bargaining for love with sex!

Homosexuals and heterosexuals are dealing with exactly the same problem, the same temptations, the same rejections and the same Word of God. This was all clearly illustrated when I was invited to a gay club in Cape Town by someone who told me, "We feel ostracised and pushed around by the church. Come and talk to us about what the Bible and the church should say and are saying about homosexuality."

When I arrived, I found I was facing five gay theologians. We engaged in good discussion, but ultimately, one cannot argue with the plain text of the Scriptures. They kept putting forward emotional, humanistic arguments, and I kept going back to the original Greek and Hebrew.

Eventually one of them got extremely frustrated with me and said, "You will never understand because you are heterosexual. You will never know what it is like for me as a homosexual to get into a bus, look at the bus driver and feel instant erotic attraction."

I replied, "Perhaps so, but you don't understand what it is like for me as a heterosexual to get into the same bus, ignore the bus driver, but then be faced with twenty attractive females sitting in the bus, absent mindedly assuming what to me are at least one dozen erotic poses! I know I shouldn't let my thoughts run riot, so I try to read my magazine, but that is full of semi-naked girls trying to sell me something through that kind of advertising. I get home, throw the magazine away and switch on the TV, but I am faced with virtually the same thing, now live. It is a lot more difficult for me as a heterosexual in today's world not to lust or engage in coital activity outside of marriage than it is for you, the homosexual, simply because I am constantly and deliberately targeted with temptation."

He had never seen it that way. He had thought that somehow I had it easy and was just being inconsiderate, not understanding his sexual temptations. But homosexuals and heterosexuals face exactly the same sort of temptations.

But to return to the original question, why do people become homosexual? What factors would influence an individual to choose a homosexual lifestyle?

To understand this more deeply, we have to look at what "scripting" is all about. On page 42 is a map of sexual "scripts", as we refer to them in sexology. What we mean by this is the outline, the prompt we all have in our mind that causes us to act and feel in certain ways. In the production of this map you see there are macro influences, subcultural influences, interpersonal influences and individual influences that all lead ultimately to the sexual script.

At the macro or global level, the social institutions have an influence. That could be religion, the family environment, a more or less strict or restrictive environment, which will influence your outlook on sexuality. It could be the economy, how much money is available to you to allow you to act out sexually. The outlook of medicine and the law play their part in your script. Then there is the sexual ideology in which you are raised. Are you brought up to see sex as procreational – a way of producing babies? Is it recreational – purely a means of having fun? Is it therapeutic – is sex good for you, and if you don't get it, do you get sick? Is it ascetic – sex is bad and the less you have, the better? Then there are the institutional structures. Is there a stable structure in the government of the land in which you act out sexually? Are you growing up in a society where there is a clear distinction between men and women and their respective roles, or is it blurred? That would all affect the scripting eventually. All of this is at the macro level.

Then there are the subcultural influences. The intergroup relations in a society, the strength of the group boundaries, be they ethnic, social, or marital. The way that gender is regarded in a society. If you are a woman, are you openly valued or looked down on? Are you the one who does the menial work and should be seen and not heard? Or are you regarded as a productive member of the society? Religion again has a part to play in making social controls.

At the interpersonal level, we have the socialisation process – parents, peers, opportunities. The accessibility to the means of developing autonomy, and the availability and accessibility to partners. How this influences scripting should be fairly self-evident.

At the individual level there is the core gender identity, which is the deep sense that one is male or female and is established by the age of about two-and-a-half to three-and-a-half years of age. That deep sense of masculinity or femininity is entrenched by this age. It has to do with a whole lot of influences on a child in the early stages of development.

All of these factors together contribute to a person's scripting. So, what would lead a person to express themselves in a homosexual way, to end up with a homosexual script? It would be one, or many more of these factors that go into making each human being's sexual script. There is no simple answer to this question because there are so many, many factors that contribute to this script.

Is celibacy the only option for a homosexual Christian?

There are doubtless many homosexuals who will argue that I am being unfair when I answer this question with an unequivocal yes. The promiscuous heterosexual can become a Christian, or if already a Christian, can repent and say that he/she is not going to be promiscuous any more, or engage in sex outside of marriage. But that person knows that there is a good chance that one day marriage will come around and sex will be on the agenda again.

However, by saying yes to celibacy for homosexuals, or perhaps homophyllics, I am condemning them to a life without sex because they are never going to get married, and Scripture forbids them to have coitus with those of the same gender. Absolutely right! And the person who thinks that is really cruel has probably bought one of the most atrocious lies of the sexual revolution, which says that coitus is something you *must* have. Sex is sex. It is not a vital need in life, although it is something very precious.

Of all the things that Scripture could use to define the relationship between Christ and the Church, the imagery describing the sexual intimacy of husband and wife is the one constantly chosen. But it *is* between husband and wife, the two who were created in the image of God, male and female. God has masculine and feminine aspects to his nature. He is El Shaddai – El, the strong one; Shaddai, the breasted one. He is a mighty warrior, but also loving like a mother.

You do not find this picture of Godhead, or of Christ and the Church, in two people of the same sex engaging in a homosexual act, because they are not complementing one another, in the same way that uniquely different males and females can complement one another. It is that masculine and that feminine complementarity that was created and divinely chosen to reflect those divine realities.

People from all walks of life can have a calling to be single, be they heterophyllic or homophyllic. There are many people who are not Christians who choose to be single because of their careers. Jesus wanted to be single. The apostle Paul wanted to be single. And if a homophyllic decides not to marry, and that he will not have coitus for the rest of his life, just like many other individuals for the sake of his vocation, calling, or whatever, then that is a momentous decision to make before God, which does not, and should not, mean the cessation of sexual intercourse or love life.

I have enormous respect for homophyllics who remain celibate. They get criticised from both sides. They are really between a rock and a hard place. On one side the Church might criticise them because they are not acting "normally" by getting married. On the other side are the homosexuals who think they are weird because they are not having sex. But I have respect for these people who lead celibate lives and yet are active in ministry, in society, and are able to love and interact with others in true homophyllic fashion.

Can a homophyllic ever become heterophyllic?

The answer is yes, if that is what he wants and feels led to by God. It is, however, very important to understand that the goal of dealing with a homosexual is not to make him a heterosexual. If a homosexual comes to me expressing the desire to somehow be free of his homosexuality, I do not encourage him to go and have sex with a female, get married or learn to lust after females. I help him understand and accept his true nature, his ability to love someone of the same sex, and learn how to experience and exercise sexual intercourse and homophyllic love, without believing that he must perforce engage in homosexual coitus. If in the process he realises that this is not his true nature, but one which developed in his bargaining with sex for love, or as a result of particular experiences or circumstances, then I help him to see the possibility of his consciously choosing to rewrite his script to conform to the one he feels led to by God.

I would do exactly the same with a heterosexual who came to me and said, "I don't want to have sex any more until later in my life, or never at all." There is no difference. Neither homophyllics nor heterophyllics are obligatory homosexuals or heterosexuals. In other words, no matter whether you love a man or a woman, you are never obliged to have coitus with them. Love and sexuality can be expressed fully for people of the same or opposite sex without any genitals involved in the exercise. Orientation and scripting are determined in many ways from birth onwards, but coitus is always a choice.

Can a homophyllic ever become heterophyllic?

Can a homosexual ever become heterosexual?

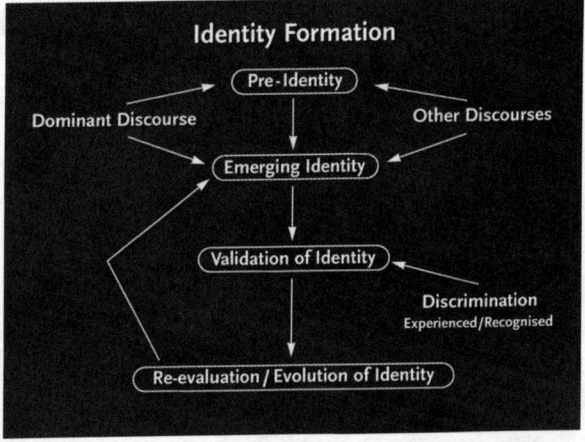

To answer this question, we need to look at the flow chart on page 58 that explains how our personal identity is formed. There are four stages.

Pre-identity

This is the stage where the individual is not quite aware that there is a label to describe him or herself. In other words, the child is not aware that there is a visible difference between himself and others. For example, you will find small children playing together, blissfully unaware of any racial distinction between them. The introverted youth may not be aware that there are others of the same age who, in comparison with himself, would be considered quite extrovert. He is just who he is. The heterosexual person is not aware that some people may have homosexual attractions. All these are examples of the pre-identity stage.

The person in this pre-identity stage has been exposed to the so called dominant discourse, that is to say, what is considered normal or standard in that society. The dominant discourse may be defined by law, medicine, the media, religion, family, and so on. However, other discourses, that is, what the individual is not exposed to, also influence pre-identity. You will hear people say, "I didn't even hear the word lesbian until I moved into my teenage years. I wasn't aware there was such a thing." Or, "No-one mentioned the colour of my skin until I moved to the city. I wasn't even aware of my blackness as a race until then."

At this stage, when an individual's visible differences, behaviours or feelings are at odds with the norm, then a subconscious sense of being odd, of being different, begins to develop. This is why you will hear some homosexual people say, "As far back as I can remember, I always felt different. Somehow, before I became aware that I had the ability to love someone of the same sex, to have close bonds with someone of the same sex, I already sensed I was not like most of my peers. The other boys were always playing rough games and I was always more tender-hearted than that, more loving, more caring."

That is pre-identity.

Emerging identity

This stage begins once abstract reasoning skills have developed. The individual begins to formulate thoughts, abstract thoughts, about the nuances and implications of the norms of the society in which he or she lives. If you ask some people, "When did you become conscious of being heterosexual?", they reply that there never was a moment when they consciously became aware of the fact. On the other hand, others would become very conscious of their emerging identity because it happens to be at odds with the norm, at odds with the rest of the world.

The stereotypes are questioned in this emerging identity stage. A young teenager who is trying to grapple with the concept of lesbianism might ask, "Do all lesbians hate men, or want to be a man?" Or the boy who is beginning to experience the effects of racial discrimination might ask, "Are all whites inherently racist?" Or the teenager who looks at television and movies might well wonder if all healthy males are preoccupied with sex, because that is what is portrayed on the screen. He is beginning to develop a male identity and is starting to ask questions about this stereotype, be it sexual, masculine, feminine or whatever.

Validation

In this stage discrimination plays a major role, because the individual who experiences discrimination will be forced to explore his identity and deal with it.

Discrimination occurs in many ways. It could be economic discrimination, denial of equal access to education, jobs or goods because of one's nationality or colour of one's skin. It may be discrimination in the form of harassment or violence, either psychological or physical, because of religion. Perhaps it is social exclusion, being segregated to certain suburbs, schools or clubs which are specifically relegated for one's group. It could be discrimination in the sense of rendering a category invisible. You happen to be a Bosnian in Timbuktu, and nobody cares about Bosnians in Timbuktu. You do not have a voice, a newspaper, anybody who pays attention to you, in fact you seem to be invisible.

All of these are ways that discrimination can manifest, but they do not always lead to a victim mentality. Sometimes they lead to activism, a reaction that says, "I'm proud of being who I am." It could be political, sexual or racial activism.

If there is no experience of discrimination, then the individual will not become consciously aware of an identity, because that person is thus not forced at this stage to validate the identity. This is why, for example, so many western white people, living in parts of Europe that are virtually exclusively white, have a poor racial identity. Being white has never been an issue to them. In some parts of the world everyone is white, or everyone is black, so colour is not an issue at all. Where I live, in South Africa, being white or black is very much an issue. In my country we are only too aware of our identity.

Re-evaluation

This stage is to do with the evolution of identity. As individuals grow through various experiences in society, they develop personal and interpersonal skills and a sense of identity. But that identity may change, sometimes gradually and in barely discernible ways. For example the man grows up and gradually changes his identity from being a carefree teenager to being a responsible member of society in the workforce, and perhaps later a husband and father.

The change can also be abrupt and dramatic. For example, the move from a healthy identity to a sick identity can happen in a flash when an HIV test comes back and says you have tested positive. You still feel healthy, but you have AIDS, and all of a sudden your thoughts turn to death. Your identity has changed from unconcerned and healthy to concerned and dying.

Being born again in Christ can have a dramatic and immediate effect on, say, the sexual identity of a homosexual, or a compulsive masturbator, or promiscuous heterosexual. That same person's identity in relation to a spouse or to society may, however, take years to change and evolve. Sometimes there is a dramatic review of a homosexual identity when a person discovers that what they thought about homosexuality was all wrong. They begin to question whether they are an obligatory homosexual or simply naturally homophyllic. If they are homophyllic, perhaps that is why they thought of themselves as bi-sexual, because they would rather have sex with females, but are able to have deep, loving relationships with men at the same time. Suddenly there is a review of that identity and the whole process begins again with a new, emerging identity.

To return to the original question, can a homosexual really change his identity to a heterosexual one? Yes, I've seen that happen. Men who were erotically attracted to men are now attracted to women. Certainly I have seen people change their understanding of themselves from homosexual to homophyllic, and coming to accept themselves as homophyllic. But I would emphasise one thing again: the goal of helping a homosexual is not to make him a heterosexual. That may be cruel and not what is desired or required. People need to understand and review their identity in the light of the difference between feelings and actions. Scripture praises someone who loves somebody of the same sex, in fact commands them to do so, but also says that just as a heterosexual does not have to have coitus with someone of the opposite sex, neither does a homosexual have to have coitus with someone of the same sex in order to express that love.

So the sexual identity can change, but when there has been a long period of homosexual activity or relationship, it is very difficult to effect that change. It is possible for a homosexual to learn to become erotically aroused by a person of the opposite sex, possible, but not an easy task. A full heterophyllic relationship with coital abstinence is often an easier choice.

The same is true for the heterosexual who, after a long period of heterosexual activity or relationship, finds himself deeply involved in a love relationship with someone of the same sex. The newly divorced or widowed growing very close to a same sex friend may experience this situation. It is possible for a heterosexual to learn to become erotically aroused by someone of the same sex and become homosexual, possible but not an easy task, and one often fraught with fear, guilt and confusion. A full homophyllic relationship with coital abstinence is often an easier choice, and of course a more Biblical one.

Homosexual to heterosexual change, and vice versa, is not at all impossible but may not be easy, especially when there has been a lot of coital activity, and especially when the sexual identity was formed and validated in early childhood.

Does discrimination **delay** identity change?

A short answer – yes, very much.

Unfortunately, the Church is often guilty of such discrimination. It is sad how the Church has repeatedly misunderstood the Biblical message and discriminated against homosexuals. If a man comes to a minister and says, "Pastor, I have sinned. I have been promiscuous, I have committed adultery", the minister might reply, "You bad boy. I want you in church twice on Sunday for the next few months and at every Bible Study, every Wednesday!"

But a person who comes and says, "Pastor, I have sinned. I am in love with a man", could well be met with the response, "Stay away from my church, from Bible Studies, and especially from the youth club."

Why do Christians draw a line where Jesus did not? He condemned the Pharisees for waxing eloquent against sexual sinners when he said, "Whoever of you is without sin can throw the first stone."

Sadly, the Church has, in effect, thrown stones and unwittingly driven people who needed to understand the difference between homosexual and homophyllic towards the homosexual camp. And what did they find there? Romance, security, companionship and love. The very things they should have found among Christians.

Jesus said, "By this will all men know that you are my disciples, if you love one another." Tragically, often all the homosexual finds in the Church is hatred and rejection, and the only place he often finds love is where the homosexuals gather. What an indictment of the Church!

Does discrimination delay identity change?

Is AIDS God's judgment on homosexuals?

It seems to be a fairly commonly held view, particularly in Europe, that because a majority of people who have AIDS are in a homosexual lifestyle, AIDS is the judgment of God on them. Where I come from, Africa, the majority of people with AIDS are heterosexual, and even in Europe and America it is moving very quickly from homosexual and drug addict communities into the heterosexual community. But wherever it is found, is AIDS the judgment of God?

To answer this question properly, we need to consider what Scripture says about different kinds of judgment, and how they relate to AIDS.

Universal judgment

Universal judgment is characterised by the fact that all men, women and children are affected. In other words, the whole earth is affected by universal judgment, manifesting itself through illness, ageing, death, toiling in work, pain in childbirth and spiritual death. All of these come to us because of the sin of Adam which brought judgment upon the world and is still manifest in all of us.

Does AIDS come under this category of judgment? Yes, because it is a disease, like many other diseases which came into the world because of sin. There was no disease when God created the world, but because of sin you can have a transfusion recipient contracting AIDS. The spouse of an intravenous drug user, or the spouse of an adulterer can give birth to a baby born with AIDS. None of those infected caused the infection directly by sinning, but simply suffered the consequences of sin in the world. AIDS is not confined to a certain type of person or section of the community. It is universal and, therefore, a part of God's universal judgment.

Cause and effect judgment

This category can be physical or moral. Physical cause and effect judgment is that which befalls people as they reap the consequences of their actions. If you walk too close to the edge of a cliff and fall off, you die! Cause and effect.

Moral cause and effect judgment is when people reap the consequences of their sin, for example, a person might become sterile having contracted venereal disease after an adulterous sexual relationship.

Is AIDS cause and effect judgment? Yes, it certainly can be, in the sense that it can be the obvious consequence of sinful behaviour, for example, living a promiscuous lifestyle. Couples who are virgins at marriage, and who remain faithful to each other, will not transmit AIDS through sex, unless one picked it up accidentally, say, through a blood transfusion. So in this sense AIDS is cause and effect judgment: the reaping of the consequences of sinful behaviour.

Specific divine judgment

This category of judgment is characterised by a number of unchangeable things. It is always directed towards a specific group of people, it happens at a specific time, and it is announced by God himself in some way at the beginning of the judgment. Examples of this are the Flood, Israel's forty years of wandering, the destruction of Korah and his followers, the drought of Elijah and the destruction of Sodom, to name but a few.

Is AIDS a specific judgment of God? No, not by that definition. It is not directed at a specific group of people, it is no respecter of class, age, race or religion. Anybody can get AIDS.

AIDS was also not specifically pre-announced by God, or declared by him to be a specific punishment for a specific sin.

Often, behind the notion that AIDS is the judgment of God on homosexuals is the belief that they do certain things that heterosexuals do not do, particularly engaging in anal sex. But sodomy is not a prerogative of homosexuals. There are many homosexuals who do not engage in anal sex, and there are a lot of heterosexuals who do.

So AIDS is universal judgment, it is cause and effect judgment, but it is important to understand and be really clear that it is not a specific judgment of God. Why is this so important? Because if Christians see this as specific judgment directed against a specific group, say, homosexuals, they would tend to step aside.

In scriptural examples of God's specific judgment, you find the righteous always humbly accepting God's judgment and stepping aside to let that judgment take its course. And if AIDS was a specific judgment, then the unrighteous might say that AIDS sufferers got what they deserved. They didn't have to be drug users, or have indiscriminate sex and pick it up from somebody else. Christians and unbelievers alike would be tempted not to involve themselves in the care of people dying from AIDS.

And even if AIDS, as a disease, is a cause and effect judgment, Christians dare not stand aside uninvolved. Jesus saw disease as an opportunity to reveal God's glory. In John 9 the disciples asked him about a man who had been born blind. "Who sinned, this man or his parents?" they asked him. And Jesus replied, "Neither, this happened so that the work of God might be displayed in his life."

And it is important to recognise that even where there was blatant sin involved, Christ's compassion often preceded the call for change. He didn't say, "You must change first, then I will help and accept you." He went out and dined with prostitutes, spent time with people, showed love, compassion and forgiveness. That is how he got through to people. He did not accept their sinfulness, he still called them to repentance, but showed them that they were loved because they had a soul worthy of knowing a Saviour.

I wonder what difference it would make in terms of our impact for truth if we fellowshipped with practising homosexuals, loved them as we would love any other person?

If we befriended drug addicts or hugged prostitutes? Perhaps then we would be able to reach out and bring a real message of hope.

Could homophyllics live together permanently?

I suppose what this question is really asking is: if you have two men who really deeply love each other, who are not having sex, who share a house, care for each other, experience romance, security, companionship, homophyllic sexual intercourse and unconditional love, could they spend the rest of their lives together?

I do not think that there is a problem with this. That is what I was alluding to earlier on when I was talking about homophyllic or heterophyllic relationships without coitus. Unfortunately we have to face hypocrisy and double standards in our mainly heterosexual society. It is what homosexuals very often and rightly label homophobia and there is often no rhyme or reason to it.

Having said that, I would say that couples who love each other, who want to live together, do also have to take notice of the world around them. They may have to be extremely careful that certain physical expressions of tenderness were not expressed in public, because they might be grossly misunderstood and it would actually be a bad witness in the society in which they live. In essence, however, what they are doing, demonstrating that two people can love each other without sex, is a good witness, a ministry in itself.

As I said in answer to a previous question, I have great respect for homophyllics who are abstaining from coitus and I do not see anything wrong with two homophyllics living together.

But I have had people, even ministers, say to me, "How can a man love a man the same way that a man loves a woman. There is something obscene about that." Of course it is possible, if you take out the lust and coital dimension. Why can a man not have the same romance with another man that he has with his girlfriend?

Jesus had a tremendously deep relationship with John. He cried at the death of his dear friend Lazarus, his heart was broken. He didn't cry when a lot of other people died, whom he also raised from the dead. He cried about Lazarus because he loved him. Jesus knew what it was to have a deep love for another man.

We would do well to become a little more Christlike and not look askance at two homophyllics who are sharing a deep, loving relationship, be they male or female.

Is the person who cross-dresses, or who has a sex change, the same as a homosexual?

In the Fourth Edition of the *Diagnostic and Statistical Manual of Mental Disorders* of the American Psychiatric Association (DSM–IV), you will find three groups of disorders under sexual and gender identity disorders.

Sexual disorders

Here we are talking about things like orgasm disorder, pain with coitus, libido disturbances, etc.

Paraphilias

Under this group would be exhibitionism, paedophilia, sado-masochism and transvestic fetishism.

The definition of transvestic fetishism would be that over a period of at least six months a person experiences recurrent, intense, sexually arousing fantasies, sexual urges and behaviours involving cross-dressing. The fantasies, or sexual urges or behaviours are clinically significant and cause distress and impairment in social, occupational or other important functions. In other words, it is interfering with the person's life. That is not homosexuality, it is transvestic fetishism.

Gender identity disorder

This disorder is when a male says, "I have a male body, but I feel like a female." Or vice versa for a female. He wants to have a sex change operation. This comes with gender identity disorder. The trans-sexual is also not necessarily homosexual, in fact, rarely so.

What comfort do you have for parents of a homosexual child?

This is something which causes a lot of heartache, and probably the place where most parents start is to ask, "Did we go wrong? Did we fail to teach what we should have taught? Did we not do what we were meant to do?"

These sort of questions are quite natural. But having come to the conclusion, "No, we did our best and there is nothing that forced our child into making these choices," let it go. Do not plague yourself with the eternal "What if?"

Do remember that you need to continue loving your child. He is still your child, a human being loved by God, and responsible to God. Although you are not taking responsibility for the choices he is making in terms of coital activity, you are still sharing with and loving that child. The fact he may be more homophyllic than heterophyllic should not be a problem to you, and, if anything, could be a cause for rejoicing in his special gifts.

How far you go in accepting the homosexual behaviour of a homophyllic son is difficult. Usually couples progress from the initial shock and rebellion against it, "You are welcome to come home any time, but don't bring any of your boyfriends with you", to perhaps being a little more relaxed and allowing the boyfriends home as well. There may be contracts negotiated on the way your son and his partner behave in your house in terms of expressing affection etc., in the same way there might be if the partner were a girlfriend.

Resist the temptation to see homosexual sin in a different light as heterosexual sin. In your society or community or family it might be more embarrassing to you, but sin is sin in God's eyes. Christ died for your son who is sinning sexually with a man, as well as for your other son who is sinning sexually with a woman. Pray for both, for both can repent and sin no more. Literature is full of the testimonies of men who stopped their homosexual behaviour and continued in productive homophyllic relationships, or even changed more radically and entered into heterophyllic relationships and heterosexual marriage. So pray for wisdom as to how to witness and continue to love your son, and pray, pray, pray.

Of course, if you realise that you did play a significant role in your child's homosexual choices you do need to ask God and your son for forgiveness. Ignorance, faulty education, overdiscipline, lack of discipline, abuse, neglect, and a long list of possible short-comings may have influenced your son's sexual script. We all have sinned and come short of the glory of God. Sometimes the consequences hurt us and others for years to come. There truly is no sin so scarlet it cannot be washed as white as snow, so repent and begin the steady task of reparation and restitution as far as humanly possible. It may not be an easy task under some circumstances, but God does desire peace and life more abundant for you and your offspring, and he never tempts you with a task you cannot fulfil, so be renewed in your mind, seek his guidance and pray, pray, pray!

NOTES

NOTES

NOTES

NOTES

NOTES

NOTES